KILLERS OF THE ANIMAL KINGDOM

GREAT WHITE SHARKS

CAITIE MCANENEY

PowerKiDS press
New York

Published in 2020 by The Rosen Publishing Group, Inc.
29 East 21st Street, New York, NY 10010

First Edition

Editor: Elizabeth Krajnik
Book Design: Reann Nye

Photo Credits: Cover Stephen Frink/Image Source/Getty Images; p. 4 Ken Kiefer 2/Cultura/Getty Images; p. 5 wildestanimal/Shutterstock.com; p. 6 by wildestanimal/Moment/Getty Images; p. 7 Andrea Izzotti/Shutterstock.com; p. 8 BW Folsom/Shutterstock.com; p. 9 Alessandro De Maddalena/Shutterstock.com; p. 11 saulty72/Shutterstock.com; p. 12 Jim Agronick/Shutterstock.com; pp. 13, 20 Martin Prochazkacz/Shutterstock.com; p. 14 Todd Winner/Stocktrek Images/Getty Images; p. 15 Willyam Bradberry/Shutterstock.com; p. 17 Alastair Pollock Photography/Moment/Getty Images; p. 18 Ondrej Prosicky/Shutterstock.com; p. 19 Sergey Uryadnikov/Shutterstock.com; p. 21 FREDERIC J. BROWN/AFP/Getty Images; p. 22 Rodrigo Friscione/Cultura/Getty Images.

Library of Congress Cataloging-in-Publication Data

Names: McAneney, Caitie, author.
Title: Great white sharks / Caitie McAneney.
Description: New York : PowerKids Press, [2020] | Series: Killers of the animal kingdom | Includes index.
Identifiers: LCCN 2018059966| ISBN 9781725306011 (paperback) | ISBN 9781725306035 (library bound) | ISBN 9781725306028 (6 pack)
Subjects: LCSH: White shark--Juvenile literature.
Classification: LCC QL638.95.L3 M395 2020 | DDC 597.3/3-dc23
LC record available at https://lccn.loc.gov/2018059966

Manufactured in the United States of America

CPSIA Compliance Information: Batch #CSPK19. For Further Information contact Rosen Publishing, New York, New York at 1-800-237-9932.

CONTENTS

GREAT WHITE KILLER

Great white sharks are known as some of the **fiercest** killers in the ocean. Not only are they the largest predator fish in the world, they are also found in many parts of the world's oceans. They eat many different animals, from smaller fish and other sharks to large **mammals** such as sea lions and seals. These sharks are born killers!

Great white sharks are known for being **aggressive**. With their strong senses, sharp teeth, speed, and **agility**, these sharks are an unstoppable force. These predatory fish are famous for putting up a fight—and winning.

It's easy to see why great white sharks are known as the most fearsome fish in the ocean!

BUILT FOR THE KILL

Great white sharks' bodies are built for the kill. They usually grow to be around 15 feet (4.6 m) long. However, some have been measured at nearly 20 feet (6.1 m) long. They can weigh up to 6,500 pounds (2,948 kg)!

KILLER FACTS

Female sharks are usually larger than male sharks. These massive females can give birth to up to 12 babies at a time. Even their young are massive at about 5 feet (1.5 m) long at birth!

Great white sharks usually have gray bodies, but some are dark blue, black, or brown.

These huge predators have a **torpedo**-shaped body to help them move through water quickly. They can reach speeds of up to 43 miles (69 km) per hour! Their tail whips side to side to **propel** them forward as their fins slice through the water. Their white belly and darker body help them blend in with the ocean water and take **prey** by surprise.

TERRIFYING TEETH

Have you ever seen a shark tooth? People often collect them and use them in jewelry. Great white shark teeth are sharp, triangular, and jagged—perfect for tearing into their prey's flesh. Great white sharks have more than 300 of these sharp teeth!

Great white sharks have about seven rows of teeth in their mouth. They tend to lose a lot of teeth. In fact, a great white shark can lose up to 1,000 teeth during its lifetime. Luckily for the shark, more teeth grow in their place. These teeth help the shark rip off huge chunks of meat from their prey.

KILLER FACTS

Great white sharks are related to an ancient shark called the megalodon. The megalodon existed more than 20 million years ago. The size of megalodon teeth means it may have been as big as a school bus!

GREAT WHITE SHARK TEETH

Great white sharks can bite down with almost 2 tons (1.8 mt) of force!

STRONG SENSES

Not only do great white sharks have beastly bodies, they also have strong senses. Their senses of smell, sight, touch, hearing, and taste are very strong. In fact, they can smell blood up to 3 miles (4.8 km) away! Their great eyesight allows them to see in dark waters. Their bodies can sense tiny movements from far away.

Great white sharks have an extra sense that we don't have—electroreception, which is an animal's ability to detect electric fields or currents underwater. **Organs** called the ampullae of Lorenzini allow sharks to sense the tiny electric currents their prey's heartbeats make. This sense only helps the shark if it's very close to—within a few inches of—its prey.

KILLER FACTS

Sharks have such a sharp sense of smell that they can find a group of seals even when the seals are up to 2 miles (3.2 km) away!

Some scientists believe great white sharks have gotten a bad rap. They say they're intelligent, sociable, and curious animals.

BORN FOR THE HUNT

Great white sharks are natural hunters. That's what puts them at the top of the food chain! They have special attack **strategies** and skills for the kill.

Great white sharks usually attack around dawn, when it is still too dark for prey such as seals to see the shark swimming below them.

Great white sharks are masters of the surprise attack. They quietly swim underneath their prey. Then, the great white shark rises up to catch its prey in its huge mouth. The great white shark breaches, or leaps out of the water, with its meal between its many rows of sharp teeth. Great white sharks rip big chunks of their prey's flesh and swallow it without chewing. The attack is **gruesome**, leaving behind a trail of blood.

A SHARK'S LIFE

Sharks are fish, and most fish species lay eggs that later hatch as live young. However, great white sharks are ovoviviparous, which means the eggs grow and hatch inside the mother and then she gives birth to live babies, called pups, shortly after. Sharks are pregnant for about 12 to 18 months. They can give birth to two to 10 pups at a time.

Great white sharks are mostly solitary animals, which means they prefer to live on their own. They only gather to mate. Great white sharks may gather near food.

Newborn great white pups are usually around 5 feet (1.5 m) long, and over 70 pounds (31.8 kg) each! They grow to be full-sized after around 10 to 15 years. Scientists believe great white sharks can live, on average, almost as long as humans do.

PREDATOR OF THE SEA

One of the scariest things about great white sharks is their range, or the area where they live. They live all over the world! You can find great white sharks in warm to cool ocean waters, especially close to coastlines.

Some great white sharks even swim into deep water, as far as 3,000 feet (914 m) below the surface. They can also swim into very cold water, thanks to a special **adaptation**. Great white sharks have endothermic, or warm-blooded, abilities. Even though sharks are cold-blooded, they can raise their body temperature higher than the water around them.

Great white sharks migrate, or move from one area to another at different times of the year, in search of new feeding grounds.

UNLUCKY PREY

Great white sharks are built to win any fight. That's bad news for their prey! This killer is on the lookout for sea mammals, such as sea lions, small whales, and even some kinds of dolphins. Sea turtles, other fish, smaller sharks, and squid are also part of the great white shark's diet.

KILLER FACTS

Great white sharks are opportunistic eaters, which means they hunt different animals depending on different factors, such as the season, area, and their age. They will also eat dead animals if they need food.

SEAL

This great white shark has found a seal to eat. Can you see the seal's flippers sticking out of the shark's mouth?

A great white shark's favorite prey is seal. Seals often dive into the sea to hunt for fish and then come face-to-face with a great white shark. Seals are social animals, which means they often swim and hunt in groups—which is perfect for a hungry great white shark.

SHARKS AND PEOPLE

More than 100 shark attacks happen each year around the world. Great white sharks are to blame for about one-third to one-half of these attacks. In different areas the number of people who die from shark attacks varies. However, people usually don't die from shark bites. Many scientists believe great white sharks bite humans thinking they are normal prey, such as a seal, and then let go when they realize the human isn't a seal. This is called sample biting.

KILLER FACTS

In 1975, the thriller film *Jaws*, which was directed by Stephen Spielberg and based on Peter Benchley's 1974 novel of the same name, was released in the United States. The movie is about a huge great white shark that attacks people in a coastal community in New England.

If sharks have been spotted near a coastline, be sure to stay out of the water until the authorities say it's okay to go in the water.

People are much more harmful to sharks than sharks are to people. Great white sharks are being overfished for their fins, which some people use to make shark fin soup. We need great white sharks because they have an important role in the ocean food chain.

KILLER FISH!

Scientists don't know everything about great white sharks just yet. They're still studying the sharks' population, migration, and **behaviors**. These sharks are certainly skilled killers, but they've gotten a bad reputation over the years.

Even though great white sharks have frightened many beachgoers, they have caught the attention of scientists for many years. Scientists are working hard to replace the fear people have of sharks with understanding and care. The law in many places, including Australia, South Africa, and California, protects great white sharks. This makes it possible for great white shark populations to grow and also helps boost tourism in these places.

GLOSSARY

adaptation: A change in a living thing that helps it live better in its habitat.

aggressive: Showing a readiness to attack.

agility: The ability to move around quickly and easily.

behavior: The way a person or animal acts.

fierce: Eager to fight or kill.

gruesome: Causing fear or disgust.

mammal: Any warm-blooded animal whose babies drink milk and whose body is covered with hair or fur.

organ: A body part that does a certain task.

prey: An animal hunted by other animals for food.

propel: To push or drive something forward or in another direction.

strategy: A plan of action to achieve a goal.

torpedo: A rocket-shaped exploding device that travels underwater.

INDEX

WEBSITES

Due to the changing nature of Internet links, PowerKids Press has developed an online list of websites related to the subject of this book. This site is updated regularly. Please use this link to access the list: www.powerkidslinks.com/kotak/sharks